AF599205

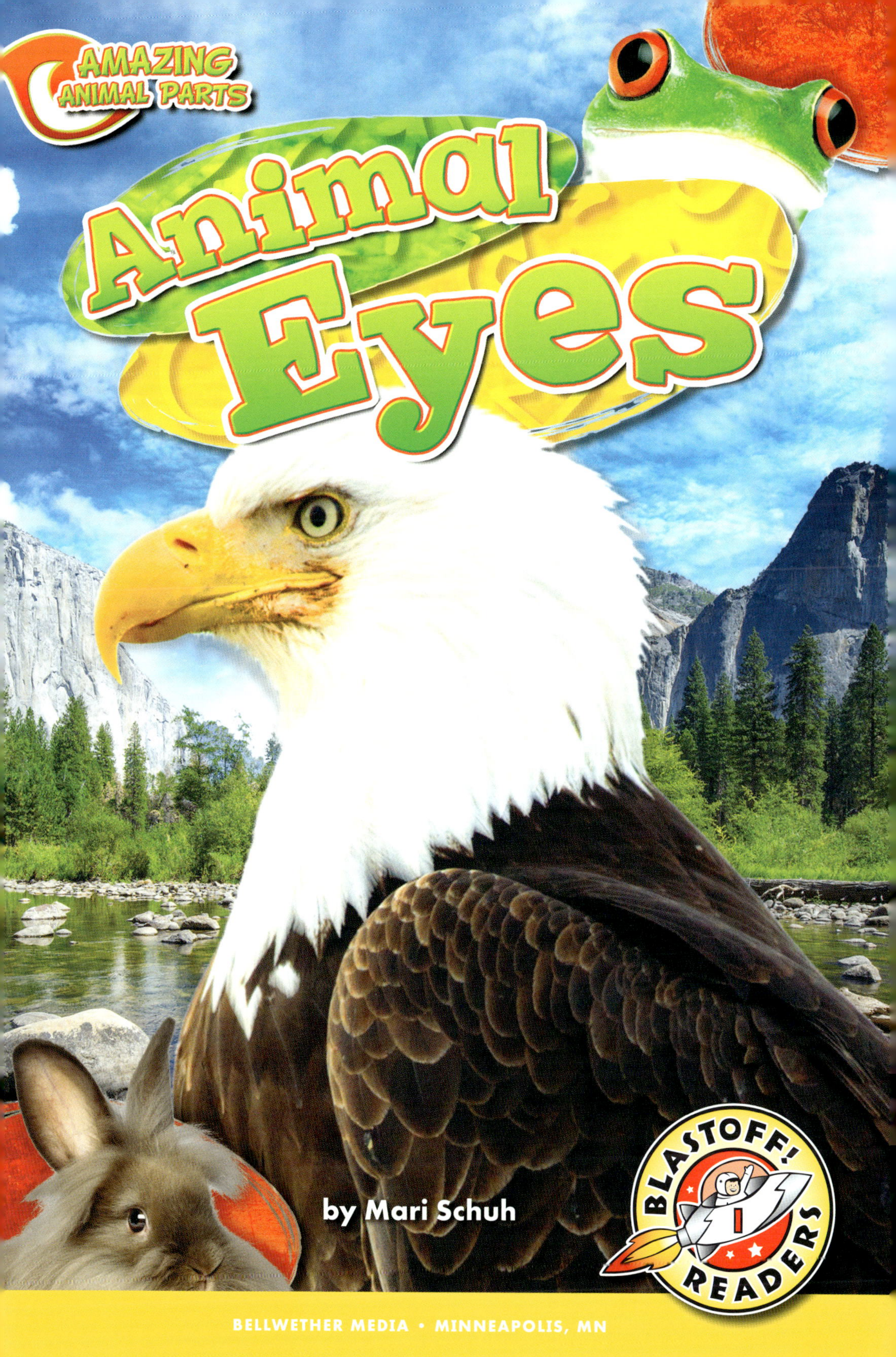

AMAZING ANIMAL PARTS
Animal Eyes
by Mari Schuh
BLASTOFF! READERS
1
BELLWETHER MEDIA • MINNEAPOLIS, MN

Blastoff! Readers are carefully developed by literacy experts to build reading stamina and move students toward fluency by combining standards-based content with developmentally appropriate text.

Level 1 provides the most support through repetition of high-frequency words, light text, predictable sentence patterns, and strong visual support.

Level 2 offers early readers a bit more challenge through varied sentences, increased text load, and text-supportive special features.

Level 3 advances early-fluent readers toward fluency through increased text load, less reliance on photos, advancing concepts, longer sentences, and more complex special features.

★ **Blastoff! Universe**

Reading Level

Grade K

Grades 1–3

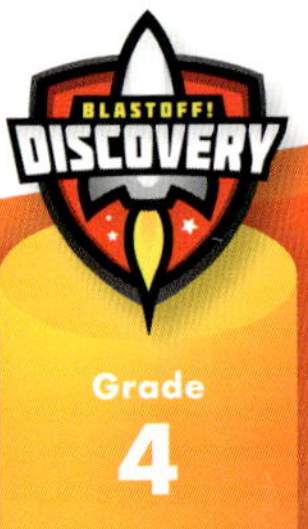

Grade 4

This edition first published in 2024 by Bellwether Media, Inc.

Library of Congress Cataloging-in-Publication Data

LC record for Animal Eyes available at: https://lccn.loc.gov/2023039765

Editor: Rebecca Sabelko Designer: Andrea Schneider

Printed in the United States of America, North Mankato, MN.

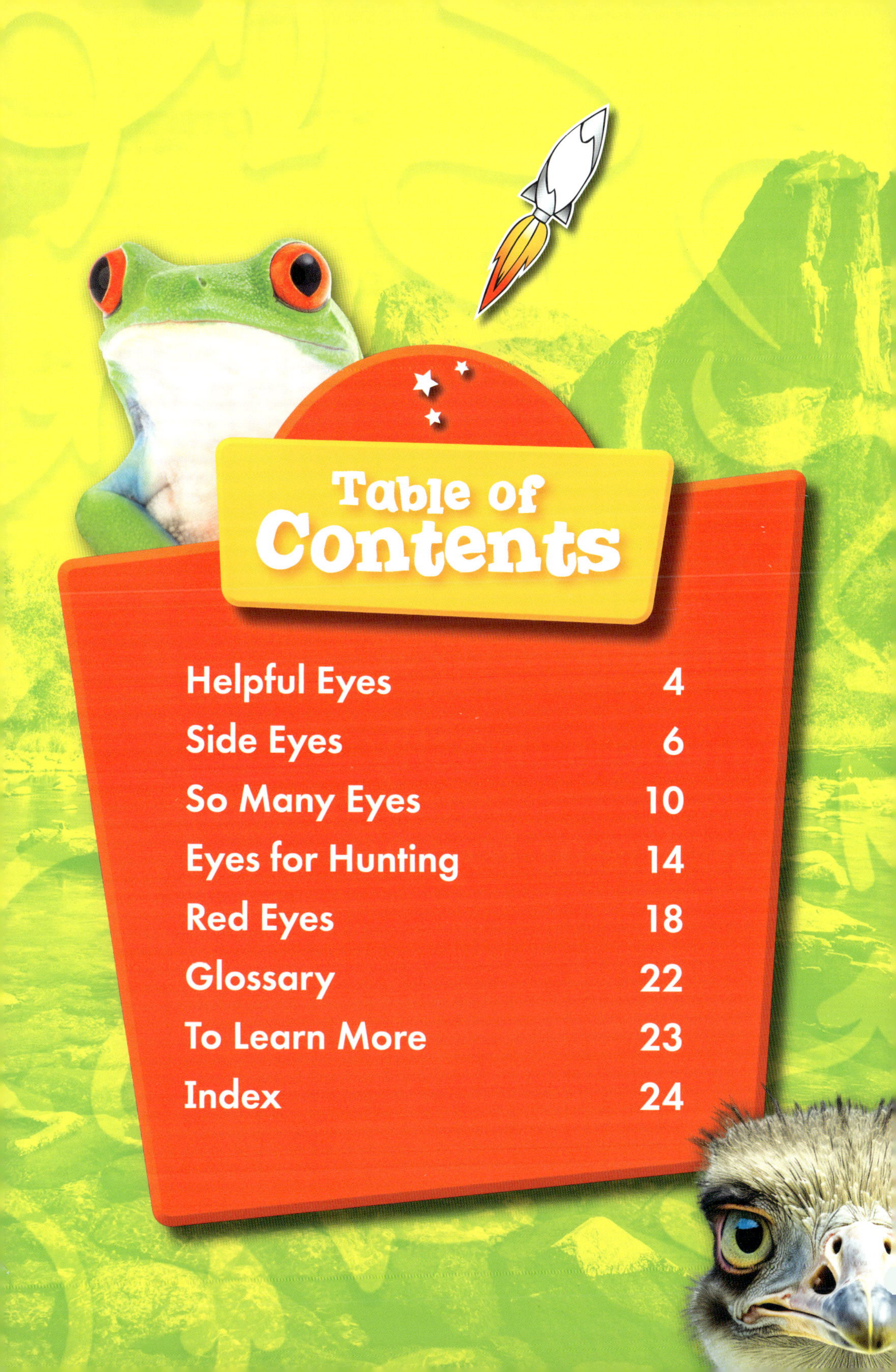

Table of Contents

Helpful Eyes

Eyes help animals in many ways! Animals mostly use them to see.

Side Eyes

Rabbits have eyes
on the sides
of their heads.

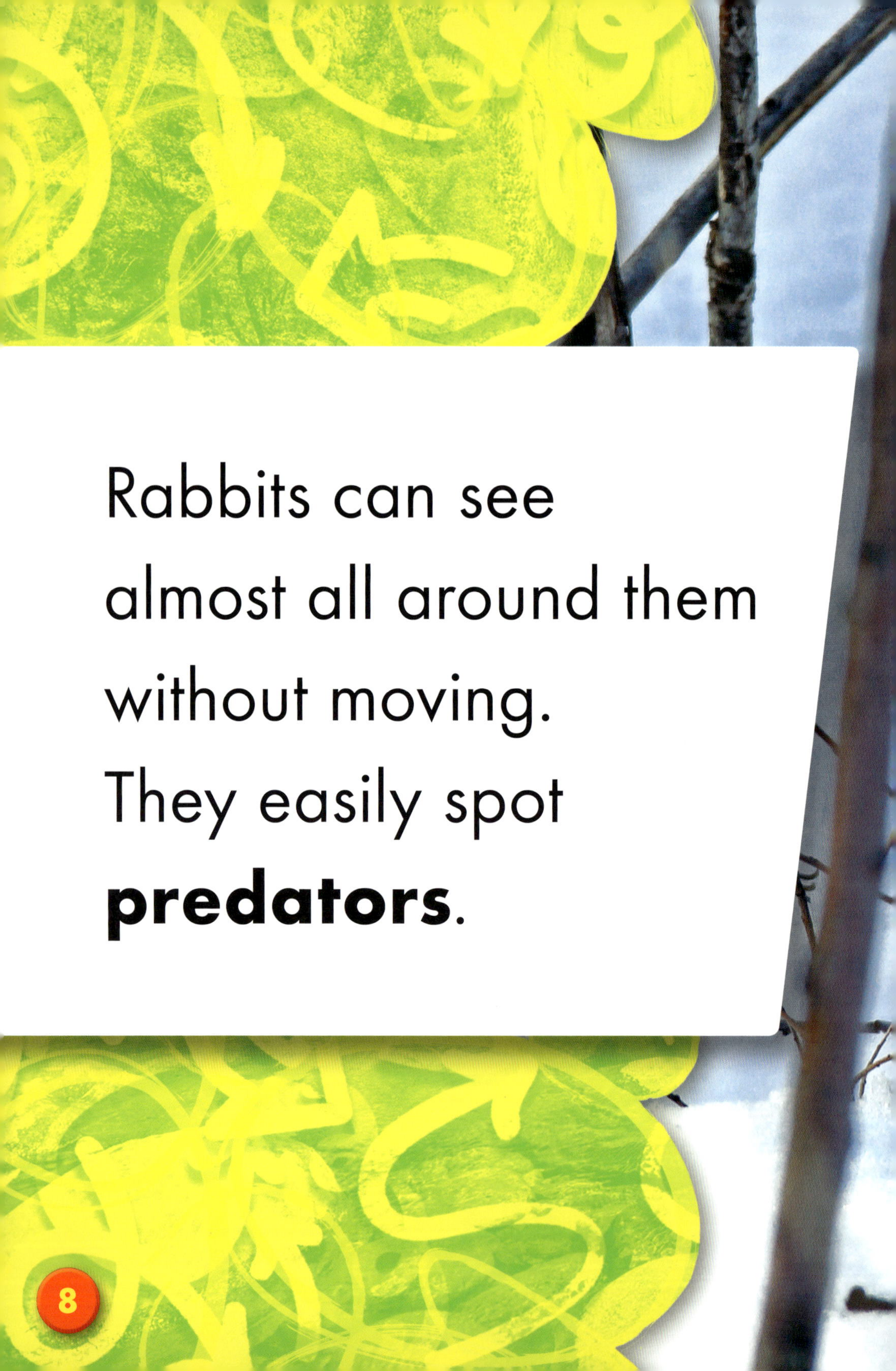

Rabbits can see almost all around them without moving. They easily spot **predators**.

predators

So Many Eyes

Sea scallops live in oceans. They have up to 200 tiny eyes!

sea scallop
eyes

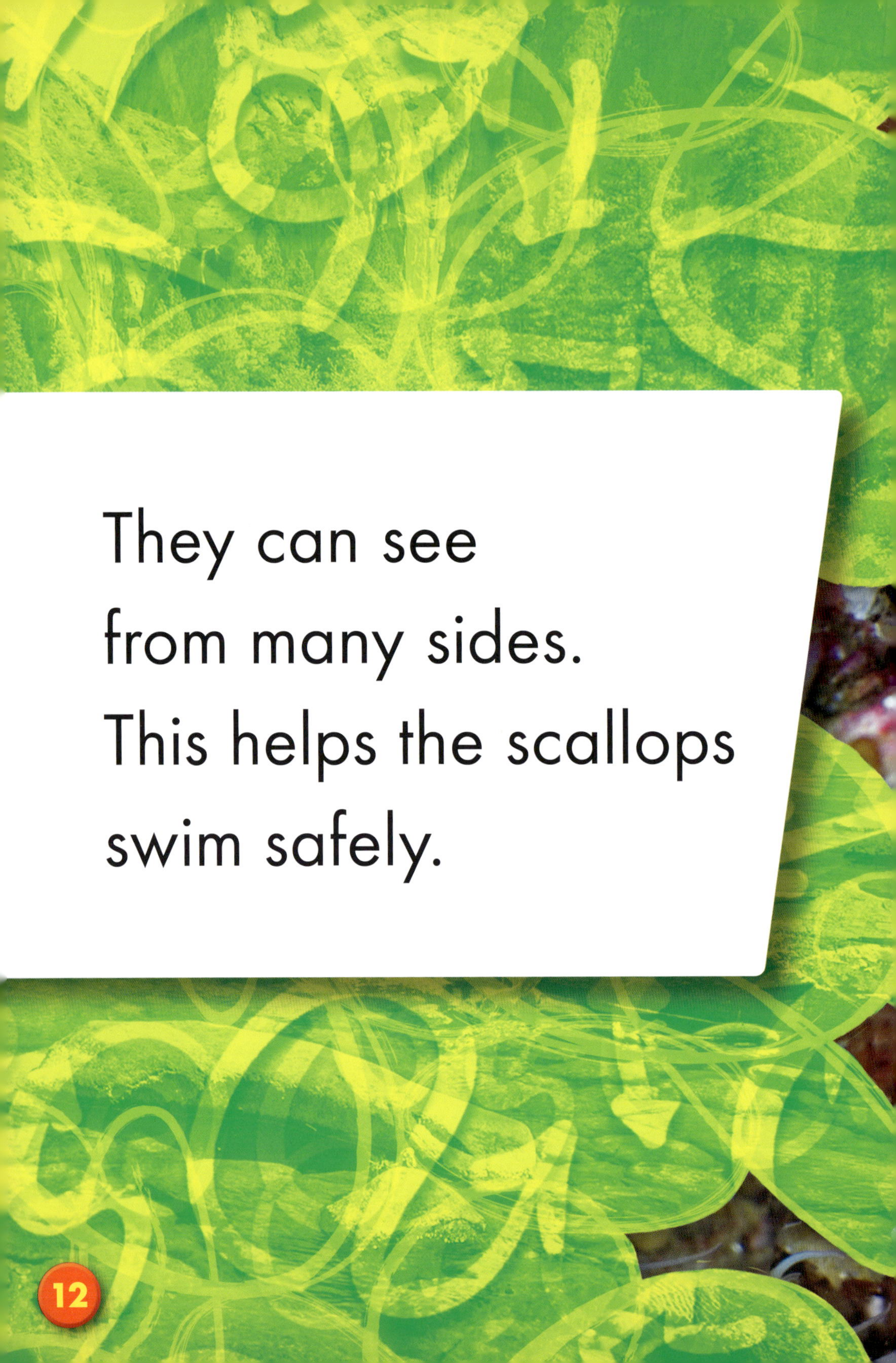

They can see
from many sides.
This helps the scallops
swim safely.

World's Biggest Eyes
colossal squid eye
around 10 inches (25 centimeters) wide
0 inches
5 inches
10 inches

Eyes for Hunting

Bald eagles can see far. This helps the eagles hunt **prey**.

prey

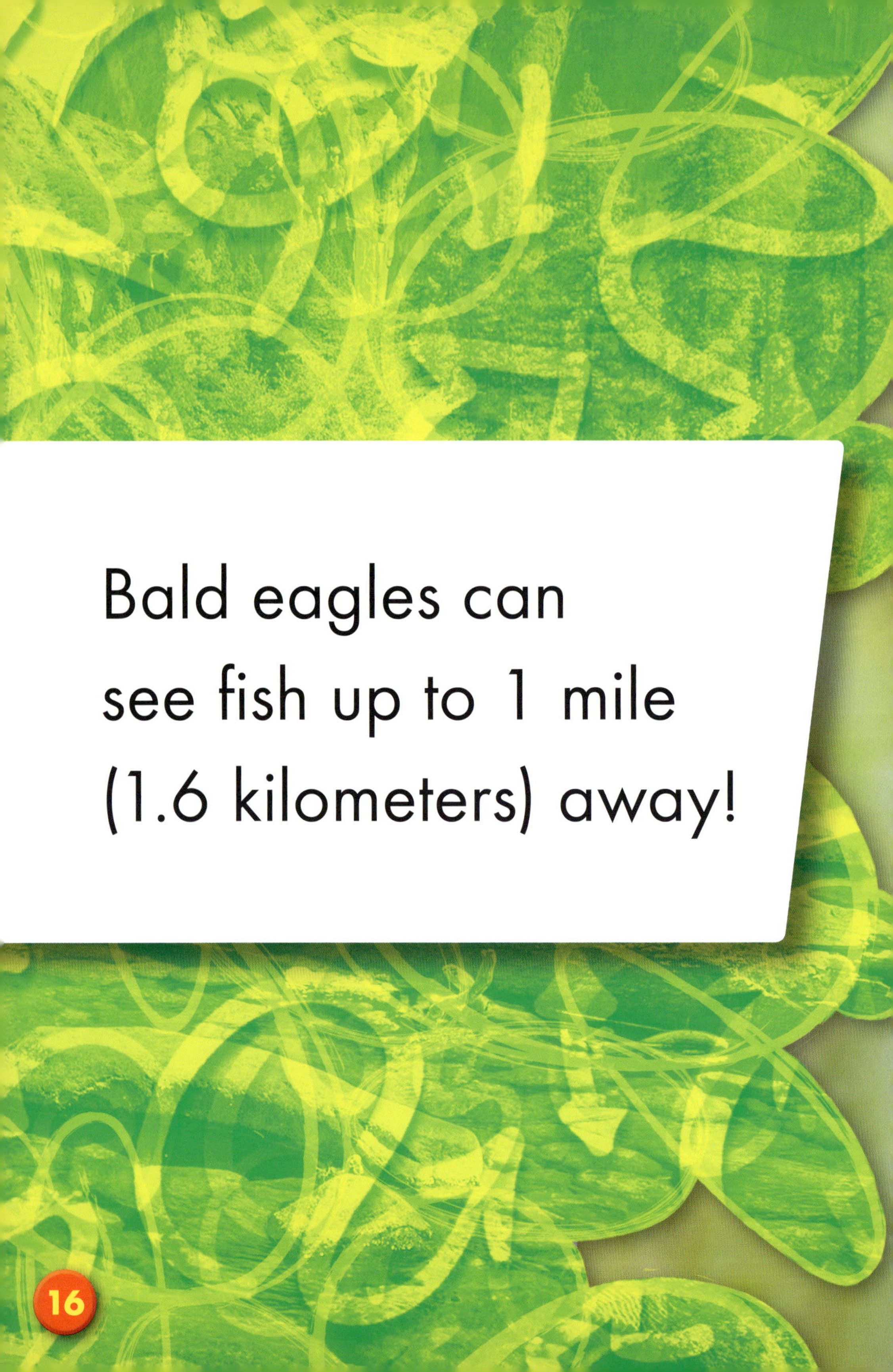

Bald eagles can see fish up to 1 mile (1.6 kilometers) away!

Red Eyes

Red-eyed tree frogs have red eyes! Their black **pupils** are up and down.

Pupil Shapes!
up and down
round
side-to-side
snake
dog
goat
pupil

Their red eyes scare predators. The frogs quickly hop away!

Glossary

predators

animals that hunt other animals for food

pupils

dark areas of animals' eyes that let in light

prey

animals that are hunted by other animals for food

To Learn More

AT THE LIBRARY

Culliford, Amy. *Eyes*. New York, N.Y.: Crabtree Publishing Company, 2022.

Griffin, Mary. *Whose Eyes Are Those?* New York, N.Y.: Gareth Stevens Publishing, 2024.

Meister, Cari. *Who Sees With These Eyes?* North Mankato, Minn.: Capstone Press, 2021.

ON THE WEB

FACTSURFER

Factsurfer.com gives you a safe, fun way to find more information.

1. Go to www.factsurfer.com.
2. Enter "animal eyes" into the search box and click 🔍.
3. Select your book cover to see a list of related content.

Index

The images in this book are reproduced through the courtesy of: Blueberries, front cover (tree frog); BirdImages, front cover (bald eagle); Mdorottya, front cover (rabbit); canadastock, front cover (landscape background); Dirk Ercken, p. 3 (tree frog); lupacoarts, p. 3 (ostrich); TheCats, pp. 4-5; Bilanol, pp. 6-7; photographybyJHWilliams, pp. 8-9; Kjetil Kolbjornsrud, p. 9 (predators); Little Dinosaur/ Alamy, pp. 10-11; ShaneKato, p. 11 (sea scallop eyes); agefotostock/ Alamy, pp. 12-13; Imran Ashraf, pp. 14-15; SaveImage, p. 15 (prey); Rob Hainer, pp. 16-17; David Havel, pp. 18-19; Kurit afshen, p. 19 (up and down); Javier Brosch, p. 19 (round); popovatetiana, p. 19 (side-to-side); Lauren Suryanata, pp. 20-21; Paula Cobleigh, p. 22 (predators); Tran The Ngoc, p. 22 (prey); Arifbello19, p. 22 (pupils); Nynke van Holten, p. 22 (owl).